'til the streetlights came on

brett alan coker

(Original Cover)

'til the streetlights came on

Brett Alan Coker

A
T.uesday's L.ife B.ooks
inspiration

<u>Series One - Book One of Nine</u>
'til the streetlights came on
(- June 1998 - October 2001 -)

Original Cover Sketch - Liesl Christman
Back Photo - Shala Anne Owen

ISBN 979-8-89379-370-3

Introduction

It's been two decades since the first words of this book were scribbled down in a 6x9 sketchbook. There was nothing fancy about the sketchbook itself; although for the first few months of me carrying it, it did have a fancy leather wrapping with leaves and shit on it. The sketchbook was stolen - not by me - from a high-end store at the mall. The kind of store that sold $250 Chinese Checkers sets, and $40 polished rocks. No horse shit.

It was a sketchbook, so there weren't any lines, Just blank white pages. The leather wrapping eventually got ditched. And thus began the first series of nine books all written in 6x9 hardbound books. Only the first two, however, were in sketchbooks. *understanding thursday* was also written in a sketchbook. For those of you not up to speed; *understanding thursday* is the follow-up book to this.

And there are twenty-five books that follow that one.

We're getting ahead of ourselves. When I began writing *'til the streetlights came on*, I had no idea what lie ahead of me. I didn't know what I was doing, or how long this fascination with writing would go. I had only recently began writing. But it was film screenplays that I started with. And somehow I ended up writing poetry. I do - and don't - recall a lot about my first writings; except to say that I am sure I cover it at some point in a subsequent book. I will say though, that my first few pieces are without a doubt lost.

The first writings - outside of screenplays - were done at Shawnee Mission East High School *[Home of the Lancers. Haha. Nerds.]* Which wasn't even my high school, but is where I went for Summer School during the Summer of 1998. Having failed the second semester of Sophomore English during the 1997/1998 school year, I had to attend three weeks of Summer School at Shawnee Mission East. And there, our teacher would take us to the neighboring park every morning or so, and have us hang out and write. And that is where I wrote my first pieces.

I either turned the writings in and never received them back; or I just threw them away. I honestly don't remember.

It truly wasn't until my Junior year, 1998/1999 that I really began to write. And while most of that writing didn't kick in 'til 1999, I will always credit 1998 as being the true origin.

1998 was a year of many firsts.
> First began to write.
> First job at a movie theatre. *(First job ever.)*
> First time I had sex.

I was sixteen years old. As I write this now, I am thirty-six years old.
Anyway.

It has been a solid ten years or more since I have read or proofread this book. But one thing that has always remained the same is the writing itself. While the formatting has changed, everything is still pretty much the same as when the sixteen-year-old version of me first scribbled it down.
I have always been very particular about chronology and leaving things as relatively raw as possible.
By doing this I hope to show growth as a writer and as a person. I have many thoughts about the things written here; but I will keep them to myself.
If you can't dislike or disagree with your thoughts as a child, then you really haven't grown up.

In this book I misuse words. I am also fairly certain that I use words that aren't even words. I use words that I *thought* were words.

I also had a big hard-on for the American Typewriter font, and not capitalizing words or using proper punctuation. What I once thought was stylistic, I now find naive and annoying.
Hopefully you can look beyond it.

This Introduction is written in my present-day preference.

Every piece is in the proper order as to when written; to the best I can recall. And nothing has been altered to make me look like *not* a fucking idiot.

This book is what it is. It's my beginning. And to alter it or erase it would be the same as trying to delete the boy I used to be. Which I would never do.
So fuck it.
Let's go.

the*BAC*
2018
West Plaza
Kansas City, Missouri

• after a name indicates that it has been changed.
* after a title indicates it is lifted from another source.

In order to conserve space and keep these books as inexpensive as possible I have allowed - when applicable - for multiple complete poems to be on a single page.

'til the streetlights came on

we're all entitled to one good scare *

he dons a mask and grabs a knife
steps into the night to end her life
it's been ten years, plus five more
since his sister's body lie upon the floor

she died that night, by his hand
he became a menace to the people of the land
he kills to cease the pain side
poor souls try to run and hide

he killed bob, annie, and lynda too
i wonder who's next, it could be you
always in search of laurie strode
he almost got her in the doyle abode

dr. loomis stopped him in his tracks
he grabbed that kid lonnie by the bike racks
driving around in a government car
dr. wynn said "oh he can't get far"

sheriff brackett doesn't believe dr. l
until michael sent his daughter to hell
from smith's grove to haddonfield
his kills won't stop nor will they yield

if you're not scared your ass should be
he's not a bitch like jason, chucky, or freddy
when annie died her head hit the horn
all because the shape is inflicted with the curse of thorn

[previously unreleased]

hypothycra

voices laugh, a bright sun rises
innocent souls await surprises
nothing to do but sit and wait
bad luck? i wish. it is my fate.

guns start blazing, choppers wail
my stomach churns, i'm turning pale
shrapnel flies, voices scream
why can't i awake from this horrific dream?

no one laughs, a bright sun rises
dead souls now, no more surprises
the rain has stopped, no more mud
my hands are clean, but i still see blood

no more grenades, whether live or dud
clean, my hands are, but i still see blood
back to the world, my wife and kid
not able to tell my son what his father did

voices laugh, a new dawn rises
no more souls await surprises
the war is over, it's finally done
i dream at night of all who's gone

my dreams at night take me back
back to the jungle when we were under attack
i think i'm back in the rain and mud
my eyes i close tight, but i still see blood

atrocity exhibition *

words fall upon deaf ears
glorious images are viewed by a blind eye
lost souls search for heaven's door
like a needle in a haystack of a bluebird sky

voices scream in pain and joy
adults, teens, and children too
voiceless screams are what they are
i scream them, how about you?

urban kids fight external stimuli
suburban kids fight the pain inside
which battle is worse? you tell me.
i truly can't decide

to fight the demon one raises a gun
          to another's face and fires
some say it's justified, but fuck all those liars
a person died to end another's pain
          however it doesn't stop
the person died in vain

internal pain is the worst to feel
there is nothing to crush
          under your shit-covered heel
internal pain is caused by you
          and also many others
you live with it for so long
          it's like you're almost brothers

words fall upon deaf ears
no one seems to care
i really don't know what to do
if i did, would i even dare?

in search of heaven's door
is what everyone seems to be
all but one have found it
guess who? that's right ... it's me.

rimbaudous importante

shapeless, formless, shaped and formed
loveless, fearless, loved and feared
hopeless, heartless, dead and cold
things i've never felt
but i am always told
the ones i'll buy are few and true
they are loveless, hopeless, dead and cold

i feel no love, therefore it's less
i have no hope, therefore it's less
inside i'm dead
outside i'm cold
my point is vague, my words are bold
this is the shit i'm always told

this is the shit i'm always told
i'm shaped and formed, and dead, and cold
i'm told and told and told and told
this trivial shit is getting old

cold and dead and formed and shaped
my heart it hurts, my mind it's raped
the truth has never really been told
the truth is this ...

a dysfunctional christmas

the door knob turns, along with my stomach
in he walks, bottle in hand
it's almost empty, yet i know he is full
the door slams, he spots me
i'm grabbed and sat upon his knee
my back he pats, my head he strokes
and in he starts with his stupid-ass jokes

seeing i don't care, he drops me to the floor
my head smashes the ground
     as the blood starts to pour
mommy rushes in, knowing what she'll see
he tosses her aside, the table smashes her knee

the belt comes flying off, i cry and i cower
in an alcoholic rage, he shows me who has the power
my skin begins to welt, some begins to tear
dreaming of a better place
     as of then it was anywhere but there

mommy rises, dad strikes down
the pain-filled screams echo through the town
the neighbors know what's happening
     and pretend not to hear
i'm sure glad i bought that belt for him
     on christmas last year

merry christmas mom, to hell with you dad
i hope you know you corrupted me
     made me full of rage
     and at the world, i am mad

enjoyed yourself i hope you did
my love you'll never have
     no matter what the bid
i'm older now and a lot stronger
you better watch your ass
     i'll take it no longer
i want redemption, i want your love
if i can't have that, i'll take your blood

a means to an end *

friends are there, but yet they're not
love is there, but yet it's not
you try so hard to see things through
people want a savior and all there is is you
    so fuck it

you open your heart to love everyone
when you need love they are all but gone
gone is what everyone seems to be
so when times get tough all you have is thee
    so fuck it

life is a bitch or so they say
that's why the pain lasts everyday
you helped them all through bad and good
you grab a gun to end it all, do you think you should?
    so fuck -

inker

once i looked at my life and i thought
what did i do to have all this pain?
i deserve happiness and love
i deserve it god damn it!
i fucking deserve it
my heart aches and i rage inside
it's hard when i am trapped
and tormented by my own mind
i have visions of the one i loved and lost
and see the one i love and will never have
why? why mother-fucker? why?
i didn't do anything wrong
i've done everything right
but i'll show you you bastards
i'll show you
i will become strong and rise again
so prepare yourselves you pricks
i'll redeem myself

_____ **new blood**

i look up as he stares down
ghostly emanations pace across my vision
my mind goes round and round

the face looks at me as if i'd always known
his empty eyes glared
in a shrill demonic tone

my heart caves in, emotions burst
i've felt this many times,
but this i swear, is the worst

hatred swelled, i could see it clear
i lied awake that night
knowing he'll appear

why won't he leave?
it hurts so much
i hate him so
he caused it all
he made me break and start to bawl

fuck i hate him god knows why
i await the day i'm saved
the day the ghost-white face dies

lamentia

god?
i hurt
it hurts so fucking bad
please tell me why. why?
i've had a good life.
i have a good family, good friends,
and a woman who loves me
but my heart is so tight and full of pain
my emotions overflow like my tears
my soul is black like my heart
visions in my mind are filled
with sights of pain and torture
what do i have to do to make it stop?
please, make it stop
please, make it stop
god, make it fucking stop!!!

apollyon

love
    peace
surrender
    peace

    i
    love
    fuck

love
    peace
    fuck it

kill me
    i rage

["apollyon" - previously unreleased]

psychopathica

dark as poe on a midnight dreary, the only light is a small glint from the corner, a tiny void which represents hope. a black viscous fluid covers the walls. blocking, partially, their smell of hatred and death. however, the jelly-like fluid harbors its own stench, that of corruption and greed. a hand punctures the small layer of skin that covers the fluid, like the skin that forms on a steamy bowl of tomato soup. the hand reaches. it reaches. my god it reaches. it searches. it searches. it searches for a base, a solid and content ground. it searches. finally it hits. a thousand miles deep. and that is the shallowest part. the shallowest part is a thousand miles deep. thousand. shallow. deep. mile. greed. corruption. hatred. hope. he retracts his tired and worn thousand-mile arm. it is now covered. now covered. now corrupted. now covered. the smell of hatred and death is branded upon him. upon him. branded. hatred. death. the smell. my god the smell. something that will never come off. nothing can ever redeem him. redeem nothing. nothing can. redeem. my god the smell. all he did was search for hope. hope. search for. all he did. all he did was search for hope, for a future, for an absolution. hope. absolution. search for. future. absolution. something he will never find. something. absolution. will never. never will. find. what is it like to be tormented, raped, and imprisoned, by your own fucking mind?

a concave scream *

falling angels with moistened eyes
distraught over the cherub's dreary demise
falling   fall   fallen   sink
no longer the blood of christ to drink
seraphim cries, serendipity departs
leaving a void in god's own melancholy heart
salvation is lost
damnation is found
they fall from his divine presence
without even
    a
    sound

verities and balderdash*

i am eighteen and i am going to graduate soon. or at least i am expected to. and if i do, then what? my whole world will change and my whole life will be different. my best friends, who i love, will leave to go off and follow their callings. i'll be here alone. thinking. remembering. reminiscing. thinking about the smell of warm oatmeal and hot chocolate after spending an hour playing in the newly fallen snow. remembering my first kiss down by the creek near my house. reminiscing about my three best friends and how we met, what we accomplished and what we can never have again. childhood innocence. riding our bikes, dreaming of girls, building mud dams in the creek. getting yelled at by our parents for coming home covered in mud.

eventually i will leave. leave the place that i have called home nearly all my life. leave behind the walls that have witnessed my growth, my happiness, and my torment. leave behind the pillows and the blankets that comforted me and caught every dreaded tear. tears that were let out over a period of eighteen painful and hate-filled years. and i will leave behind my parents. two people who have always been there through those eighteen years, but whom i've never really known. what did they enjoy? what interests do they have? how did they feel when i disappointed them? am i a disappointment? will they love me forever? i know i will them. should i tell them that? do they already know? i'll tell them again anyway, they deserve that. i just hope that the new life that i begin will be as diverse and adventurous as the one i lead now and also that i can someday show my own kids the same amount of love that my parents have shown me.

green eggs and damned, sam i am

tempestuous? i had reasons
willful? on things good and bad
everlasting love. found. will it fade?
never knew what i wanted
took everything day by day
you all know how i feel. don't you?

friends listened. but never understood
or if they did they never acted
usually i'd withdraw. helping hands?
      ask for? i never did
relationships. started.
      wanted continuance. never got

because of that i died
right away? no
eventually? maybe so
truthfully? yes
truthfully. yes

near my demise i am
over and over again i rage

money, i had. friends, a few. happiness, no
over and over again, i rage.
      my emotions i never show
rites of the last, soon i will hear
every day i wait for that certain age, the age that i fear

phoenixonica

decrepit stars in a devilish sky
streams of crimson flow, it's a time to die
angelic harps, golden-hued, broken strings
an azure soul, full of rage, evil things

a raped mind, filled with pain, hate and fears
i'm tired of this shit, fuck it all, no more tears

heaven doesn't want me
hell must prepare
to witness this man of sin
to whom no one can compare

heaven, i don't want
hell, too easily subdued
perhaps i'll find redemption
mend my strings

on the harp
        angelic
        golden-hued

a child's lament
father,

i was just wondering why you hate me? i know i mess up, but i need guidance. you act as if everything i do upsets you. and it is like no matter how hard i try or how good a job i do it will never be up to your standards. but i've tried, i've always tried, and i still do try. when you yell and hit me i don't understand why. i don't see how beating me will change who i am. all it does is eat up everything good that i have inside. it's like you hate me because you don't want me to turn out like you, or that you want me to be better than you. how can i accomplish that when every chance you get you tear me emotionally down into nothing? i strive to do all i can, and i need your support to do what you've always dreamed i could. but why do you still hate me, when i love you?

son

the carnival has closed, years ago*
i look back over everything that i have done in my life and out of those thousands of things i've done i can still remember the day i lost my way. the day i was corrupted. the day i became a puppet, with the world and all its perversity as my master. guiding me. teasing me. taunting me. using me. from that day forth i knew it would be a downward slope. and it has. from that day i realized how sick and demented our society as a whole is, and how easily a child's mind can be raped of all its optimistic thoughts. i lost my way that day. i've been struggling to find the trail and get on track. no luck yet. i look back on that day and all i vividly remember is the doctor saying, "it's a boy." then he smacked me. what a great start.

shattered in the head *

what the fuck is wrong with me? how can i be such an asshole? i
don't know why i did it, i just did. i'm a man i have to indulge myself.
it is expected.

shut up, that is bullshit! you are just looking for a way to be guilt-free
and by doing that you are disgracing her ten times more than you did
by committing the first initial act.
 i know that.
 do you?
 yes, i do.
 prove it.
 how?
 by telling her.
 i can't.
 why can't you?
 i love her too much.
 that is no reason not to tell her.
 it's not?
 no, that is the one real reason to tell her.

and what will that accomplish? nothing. i'd get a clear conscience,
but what would she get? another broken heart. another man she
loves cheating on her and a big slap in the face as if all of this was her
fault. that is how she'll see it. since both of her last boyfriends
cheated on her, she will think she is doing something wrong, when she
is not, she is actually the victim. she doesn't deserve any of this. and
i don't deserve her.

is
she
watching
me?

no.

does
she
know
me?

no.

does
she
want
to?

no.

can
i
still
love
her?

yes.

_____ **damnation**

love
death
  fear
    hate
      fear
        death
          love
            hate

do
  whichever
    it's your own fate

i
  love
    fear

i
  hate
    death
i
  also
    love
      the
        fear
         of
           taking
            my

       last

       breath

throughout my life i've battled. battled to show who i am. battled to overcome hardships and also fear. there was always this ambition and drive in me that made me push on and strive to find whatever it is that is "calling." but as the song says, "i can't keep from falling."

the life i thought i'd live i had always thought would be adventurous, yet rational and safe. well, i've come to find no adventure, many irrational actions and many unsafe situations. however, i seem to be content with that. at least at this point in my life i am. but that will change, hopefully.

i've tried many things in my life because i felt this need to. i always quit before i excelled at it though. i thought that these things were my calling.

but i am hopefully going to change. no scratch that. i am going to change. i now will have a new outlook on life. i'll see the world from a whole new perspective. i'm "through the looking glass," "i've taken the last train with velocity and passed my own death." i'm taking any and all chances that are thrown at me. and do you know why? because baby

"it' on!"

a horrorshow ptitsa

a tearful sequel

she sits there
i see her
does she see me?
what is she thinking?
with her beautiful brown hair
does she see me?
no
that's okay

i still love her

in the doorway nightly sits*

there is a song i hear, i don't know the name. the chorus goes, "you can not save me, i can't even save myself, so just save yourself!" those lyrics, when i first heard them, sounded so selfish. telling someone that you can't and won't help them is such an irresponsible thing to do. however, the chorus does make a true statement. it has become a mentality that i now condone. all my life i've helped everyone, as much as i could, and i've always tried to love everyone. but through it all i have contracted everyone's depression and pessimism. their outlooks on life are now mine. i feel everyone's hurt and know everyone's pain and i am filled with rage and anger produced by everyone's hate. everyone has done this to me. i'm their clear-conscience, i'm their salvation. they wipe their guilt-stricken and shit-covered heels on me, because i am their fucking floor mat. and now they are free. and now they are free. helpless. helpless is what i be.

"so i'll just save myself!"

angel all fire *

"mother, please forgive me. i just had to get out
all my pain and suffering. now that i am done
remember i will always love you ...
i'm your son."

"daddy" - by
korn

mother i am sorry. i've never truly appreciated you. always took you for granted, i did. it has taken me eighteen years to realize what you have done to raise me in a good environment and nurture me to the point where i can be independent.

i've told you i hate you, and called you a bitch. i didn't mean it, you know i truly didn't mean it. it is just that i rage, and have so much pain and anger bottled up inside. and when i erupt it is usually directed towards you. simply because you always happen to be there when it comes out. you are always there and have always been there. that is what i just realized, no matter what i do or say to you, whether or not you deserve it, you have always stayed by my side. and i vow, that from this day on, i will stay by yours.

salvation through the flow of ink

for me, personally, i have struggled against silence for about two years now. my brother left my house to begin a career in the military. i'm happy for him, don't get me wrong. it is just that i never would have imagined that him leaving would put such a huge void in me. when he was here i could always talk to him, there was hardly any time when i called upon him to talk and he couldn't. after a month of him being gone i felt i must do something to fill this void. so i did.

writing. more specifically, writing film screenplays. i used this to create people to have conversations with. i could write one person's dialogue and become a whole different person to respond. by doing this i created a whole new world of friends, enemies, and events. at some points they were more interesting and eventful than i was. i looked at it as my way of escaping silence. i've never been a big fan of silence. you usually have to be alone to be silent. and when you are alone, all you can do is think. you think about problems and people and how you've been hurt and how your life could be better. i wrote about my problems in these screenplays as a way to pass them off onto someone whom they wouldn't really hurt, that way i wouldn't feel so low. because if you are alone and feel sad that is when your head becomes clouded with thoughts of self-pity, low self-esteem and eventually self-termination. and that really isn't good. so in a way, writing helped me vent my pain and hatred and in some respects saved my life.

the hanging garden *

i could never truly understand that in order for me to feel any sort of love i have to be experiencing some sort of pain. well, at least to an extent.

when i was young i was always getting into trouble, and of course i would feel extremely guilty about it. but the worst part was that i would be scared to death that my father would find out. because if he did and what i did was really bad then i was in for some heavy beating. most of the time i'd get hit with "big brown" my father's favorite belt. which happens to be the belt that i hate the most, but that is understandable. while being beat i could think of nothing but the pain, then when he was done and i was trying to recover i would then think about what i had done and why is was wrong. but that changed.

my father stopped using the belt as a form of punishment, and at first i was happy, but strangely as years went on i actually began to miss that fucking thing. as i get older my life is going to change a lot more, and to be honest i know that most of those changes are going to be for the worse. my life now is completely different then it was when i was ten. i wish i could go back to those days of pain and a thousand tears, because i was secure then. i knew who i was and where i ranked in the scheme of things. but now i feel, quoting Robert Smith of The Cure, "shapeless in the dark again." meaning that without constant reminders of the higher powers above me i feel that there is no one that can stop me. but that is not true.

back to my original point. i have always been saddened by the fact that i am getting older.
i want to go back to playing kick ball.
i want to go back to sweet innocent kisses with the neighbor girls.

i want to go back to watching 'Heathcliff', 'Voltron' and 'Thundercats', every saturday morning.
i want to go back to my 'Star Wars' C3PO's cereal and my 'Dukes of Hazzard' pajamas, and my 'He-Man' big wheel.

i want to go back to those things because i found happiness in them. now all of the happiness i find is in the memories of past events, and strangely i am sometimes only happy when my father is yelling at me. because only then do i feel acknowledged, shaped and never in the dark.

heaven isn't too far away*

content? never
happy? hardly ever
a believer in god? what for?
a believer in myself? not anymore
one who hates love
one who loves hate
an asshole? so
a hypocrite? no
a fan of mainstream things
a follower of dogmatic law
a nice guy all around?
more like the type you'll emotionally tear down
attractive, popular, handsome, debonair
smart, funny, loquacious, fair
content? never
happy?

someday

it's a lewis carroll evening

as i look into his eyes i can tell almost everything about him, more than he wants anyone to know, and even more then he knows himself. his name is demption, r.e. demption. when asked what his initials stand for he'll reply, "i'll tell you sometime," but he never will. he is a white male, late teens, dirty blond hair, which is clean most of the time. his body is slightly built, but tall and lanky. his clothes are not brand name, they are all he can afford. he wants to look like the other kids at school, with their fifty dollar shirts and their expensive pants, but he doesn't want to conform. large bags hang under his sullen eyes, you can tell they have seen sights that he wants to forget but never will. his hands are baby smooth, but also seem worn and tired, his mouth is soft and pouty. as if it were meant to be full of sweet comments, but all that ever comes out are words meant to harm.

he is greatly educated, but he doesn't find education that great. he has had enough but they, whoever they are, don't seem to think he has had enough to survive. he has money but spends it unwisely, it is spent on things he feels he needs but serve no real purpose, but just to have. born into a low income "proud to be white trash" family, he moved to the suburbs to try and fit in with society. on the outside he seems the same, but inside he is different than the whole bunch. he likes to visit places that instigate memories, he loves to reminisce. he hates visiting places that instigate memories, because they make him reminisce. reminisce about the past, a childhood of pain and torment, and just all around bad situations, ironically he hates places he loves.

he loves to write. he finds salvation through the flow of ink. his smooth, tired hands help him vent his frustration and anger, but not enough. religion doesn't matter to him. god does not exist in his eyes, and if he ever thought that god did exist, then he must be dead now. his rationale on that comes from the basis that if god were real or alive, then why would he let people suffer like he does. he trusts in the government, but not fully. he finds some things they condone wrong, but as a whole they are all right. he believes that the government is not corrupt, but there is corruption in the government. he has ambitions, mainly to make a difference, somehow. he has secret desires, but they are so secret that he doesn't know. death is not something he fears, except he fears dying without knowing love, dying unimportant and dying alone. overall he is the sweetest guy you can meet, but in most situations he finds himself in he has to be a bad mother-fucker, or at least act like one. his flaws greatly outnumber his good points, the main flaw he has is that he is too attached to the past, and he looks towards the future with cautious eyes. one of his strengths is that he can listen intently, and he has enough manners to look you in the eye. this whole time that i have been looking at him he has not broken eye contact. which is probably because i'm looking in a mirror. his name isn't r.e. demption, but that is something he seeks.

gold spike

born with a name that didn't stand out
raised in suburban contract housing
sometimes forgetting which one was his
not two good with puntiation, gramur or speling
forgets to capitalize letters on occashun
like frost, he frequents the road less traveled
wants to capture every moment
sees beauty in trivial things
finds more color in black and white
makes mysteries from single frames
sees himself as a boy
when watching this boy on the tracks
the tracks less traveld

reign dear games

red fades to green, green fades to amber
and amber fades to blue
bing plays loudly on the phonograph
muffled voices laugh and cheer
you dream of eggnog instead of lukewarm beer
the tree begins to slouch as the lights barely twinkle
you have no bing to play so it's vanilla ice
also known as rob van winkle

the windows freeze over as the white snow falls
singing by yourself a sorrowful "deck the halls"
staring at the presents that reside under the tree
no anticipation in your heart
because you know what they will be
you bought them all and all for you
none will fill the void in your heart
that is reserved for a love that's true

next door the crowd cheers, as you drown in tears
a woman joyfully screams
and it shatters your thoughts, your dreams
you wonder what happened to those days of old
as you sit alone and thinking
your fingers and heart turning cold

red fades to green, green fades to amber
thirty fades to fifty, fifty fades to eighty
and it all fades to black

decepticon

a faint stench of lemonheads fills my nostrils
as i look upon this boy
his do-it-yourself haircut
'Voltron' shirt worn to shreds
the shirt partially tucked into a pair
    of acid-washed denim jeans
    that look twenty years old
black ripped Converse all-stars
    with 'Ninja Turtle' lace-fasteners
    are on his feet
looking at his face we see pain and sorrow
remnants of sadness left after the loss of a loved one
a tear runs down the side of his nose
    and over his kool-aid mustache
    to his innocent trembling lips

millennial lamentation

i stand alone, the world spins round
the world revolves around
around everyone
but me
i look, i wait
        to see
        what he
        god, has in store for me

i stand alone, people encircling me
        they laugh
what for? at who? why me?
i tell myself we're all the same
my troubles are mine
no one else to blame
i rage, i choke on my own hate
i choke, i rage about choices i made
i offer help to those in need

when i need help
no one but me

vertigo
        i suffer from
spinning world ensues
i'm tired there is no one
no more
no more
no ...

power of perception

gorgeous? course i am. look at this ass!
my self-esteem and confidence is hella good
i love everyone and everyone loves me
once again, look at this ass!
i have everything i want and need, and can get
what i don't have if i want
i don't need assistance or help of any kind
i know all and feel no pain

i am not telling the truth

clockwork enigma

bellows in the night awaken my divine eyes
father midnight croons
timid souls arise, i know why they've come
to take me back to the place i'm from
my wings take shape, my beauty blossoms
for now i swoon

entity

divinity is on my lips on this day of hope
i feel as if i'm floating
the world is beneath me
the sky is my home
the birds are peers
peers that encourage nothing
but purity
i no longer dream
my dreams are now reality
they have taken over my life and heart
i float not knowing what's ahead
not caring, not fearing, not fearing
fear no longer controls me
love and hope ensues
i'm free

unsane

screams
      the falling of angels
childish shrills
      the losing of innocence
the passing of an era
    it hurts
calm tides recess
      into the voids of my mind
pushing back thoughts of tyranny
    genocide   martyrdom
horrific thoughts cut through my mind
      like a razor amidst cocaine
cutting until it hits
the reflective surface of the mirror
in this mirror i see myself

yet, it is not me
      it is what i have become
      a mere shadow of my former self

a vision i'd like to shatter

paradoxica

morning dew drips, pooling resources
for the final battle
the army of mortal hell rises
fighting narcotic hordes of barbiturate serpents
pulsating veins of crimson light
overtones of dark are brighter
       than the burning of daily flesh
sulfur odors tickle the hairs
       make them dance
a perpetual waltz of castratos
pasty, flaky skin absorbs, the golden flow
my pupils overcome
       shining like the sun
brighter
longer
dying by my hand

       full of blood-dipped roses

lately i've been thinking a lot
trying to recall the moment that changed me
not from being immature about sex
    to respecting it
but from not caring about
    the outcomes of situations
the moment i stopped giving
    a flying fuck
i'd always wanted to have that
    "fuck it all" attitude
    but could never attain it
i've narrowed it down to two possibilities
the first one being when my father told me
    that he was divorcing my mother
the second was the time
    i had three guns pointed at my head

elaborating on the first one
my father out of nowhere
    told me that he was leaving
    and getting a divorce
this was the day i was raped
    in a sense
you see
    nothing came of it
    and they didn't divorce
he never said anything again
i was so fucking enraged
    and saddened by this
then after i got over it
    and realized it wasn't going to happen
he announced it again
again, feeling that tearing of my heart
again, nothing coming of it
my parents are still together
i was in 7th grade when that happened
imagine growing up
    knowing full well
    that your parents don't love each other
they, my parents,
    raped my mind of
    all its optimism

one night at 3 a.m.
        my friend Luke and i got pulled over
        coming home from k.u.
my friend Tim's sister invited us out
        to have a small party
drinking party
        of course
good thing
        i don't drink

a friend T.J.
        was following us back to o.p.
        'cause he didn't know how to get there

we took 32 through bonner springs
my brake lights were fucked up
they were bright all the time
        so you couldn't tell
        when i was slowing down
this caused him to ride my ass
        all the way
we were going about 90 or so
        when the lights started flashing
they were behind T.J.
        so i kept going
well, mother-fucking T.J. kept going too
so the cops followed us
        for about two miles
so we finally pulled over

i stopped the engine
        and threw the keys out the window
and as i stepped out of the truck
        i heard a pig (cop) yelling
        "take off the coat!"
i had my black trench on
        and it was fucking freezing out
i took it off
        and froze my fucking balls off
i got on my knees
        and they handcuffed me
        and tossed me to the freezing-cold asphalt

that's when i saw they had
        three guns pointed at us
T.J. was beside me on the ground
        he was kind of freaking out
        and i was telling him to chill
the cops then noticed Luke
        and fucking spazzed out
        by going over there
        and pulling him out of the truck

i got a fucking ticket for defective brake lights
        and not yielding to safety vehicles
        but i didn't get anything for speeding
i only got fined for stuff that would
        have occurred after they
        turned their lights on
the fucking pigs had
        no reason to pull us over

my point of this story
        is the guns
i had three guns
        pointed at me
in a second my life
        could have ended
it was up to my actions
        to determine whether
        i lived or died
i was closest to death
        than i ever was before
realization came to me
        telling me that i was mortal
        with higher powers controlling me
so if i could come close to death
        for small-ass shit like this
why should i give
        a shit?
i no longer do

fuck 'em

[previously unreleased]

the asphalt hourglass

love enthralls
nightly demons dance
blackness covers silver tiles
no more gleam or shine
drips run down, streams will flow
surrealistic sights and sounds
    a head hunter's toy land
like alice in the mirror
    like eeyore's broken tail
i seek fantasies, seek dreams
    visions surround, but no truth

wonderland is gone
pooh is cast aside by chris robin
pan grows old as emerald city crumbles

fascination, wonderment
    dreams of childhood dissolve
the soles of ruby slippers worn thin
i hold the pail as the witch melts
i destroy the visions of my past no longer needed

yet, i love them
the stories that spark my creativity

like the fire on scarecrow's arms

_____ **deceived**

the guardian
holds me back
hands on mine
guiding me, protecting me
not for all good

i respect its help
but don't need it
i struggle to break its grip
days into weeks
into months years

i conclude that i can not be free
the grip is released
i look back
nothing
        but my own hands

_____ **morningside**

disgraced and disowned
my mind deceives me
dancing in my psyche
angels with golden slippers
tap on velvet lakes
harmonious voices ring on
echoing through the satin streets
the absence of color invites my shining soul
to repent and share
        psychotic breaths
the last breath of cursed laments
dying
        are my words
dying
        is my soul
i eulogize my funeral
i bury myself
        by hiding emotions

it's quite interesting how you change as you get older
remembering back to my younger days

when outside with the neighbor kids
        we always had to be home
        a few minutes after the streetlights came on
when it got dark
        we could no longer leave
it is almost a complete one-eighty now
i rarely leave my house
        until after it's dark
it used to be
        "stay in the neighborhood"
now it's
        "stay in the city, or country
        for that matter"

i sometimes miss childhood
and wish i could go back
        but still knowing things i know
go back to those years
        as the person i am now
        & not who i was

it's true to be said
        that i won't enjoy
        being young again

but it's worth a shot

[previously unreleased]

_______ sanctity in awe

perplexed thoughts engulf my virgin mind
stealing its innocence
    scarring its beauty
cycloning nightmares
silky webs, spun of hate
a pool of memories
flat as a board
crystal and reflective, a mirror
blades cut through it, ruining it forever
i glide, happy, free
    ruining it, forever

attain freedom, achieve salvation
deteriorating my past, its glory
    its sadness, i glide
    happy, free
deteriorating   past
    glory   my sadness

spun of hate

_______ denouement

feeling the sadness of loneliness
feeling sad and lonely
feeling sad
feeling lonely
feel sad
feel lonely
sad
lonely
feel

darwinology
gravitational strengths
        of never-ending
        never-dying forces
a world of failure
        and myriad problems
looking at this
        i laugh
my heart turns to blue cobalt
eyes glass over in onyx
        i laugh
before i inject the serum
        of redemption

reverse in power
The Man supports me, supplies me, backs me
        The Man
"Open up, free your mind," he says
He hands me the paper, the feather
        & the bottle of blood ink

"Save yourself through writing," he says
        The Man

I open up, bare it all, save myself through writing
"That's great," he says
        Thank you
"Too bad I can't let anyone read it," he says
        Why? I ask
"Your words are your heart & soul, your life, it's
too real, that may be offensive," he says
        The Man

Thank you, I say. You broke off the tip
        of the knife in my side. I open up
        to be shut out. You've killed me.
        The Man.

["reverse in power" - previously unreleased]

traveling back almost a year
    & some change
    august '98
a new girl started working with me
    at the movie theatre
    her name was Eliza
she was a vision if i ever saw one
she was pretty in the face
    and had an excellent body
so being as we were
    all of us westglen guys
we were walking hard-ons
    around her
all hitting on her and shit
she probably got sick of it
that is when i realized that i needed
    to stop hitting on her like everyone else
i also realized that
    i fell in love with her
we talked and soon became friends
the type where we could talk about anything
    especially sex
i listened intently, ya know,
    playing the role of concerned guy
all the while using her image as a source
    for masturbatory material
however, even with our good friendship
    she fell for a friend of mine named Kris
and i was jealous of course
but actually it was his turn
    because he liked Mandy a lot
    & i got her
and i got Karen
    before that

knowing what my limits were i backed off
    and watched them get together
meaning they would stay in the parking lot
    until about 2 a.m.
    eating muff and giving head, ya know
me still jealous
Eliza was not a very conservative girl

yet she was a virgin
but not a picky one,
            she wasn't waiting for marriage
            or the right guy
just the right spot
            and the right feeling

in one sense it was like
            Kris and i were both dating her
i would talk to her and go to movies with her
            and be cordial

            and he got the blowjobs

but i'm not regretful
i knew more about her than
            most of her friends
            & that meant a lot to me
eventually opening up more and more
            to each other
then we started to learn things
            neither of us really wanted to know
my burning desire for her
            and constant fire in my loins
me wanting to shag her silly
            and her happy adventures with Kris
one time even adding an asshole
            named Ricky to the mix
            three-way time
she didn't like Ricky
            she just wanted to
            get with Kris

her and i had our tough times too
her just wanting friendship
me wanting her to
            see the chemistry between us
then one day the roof caved in

i was nice and let Kris go home early
            (this is june 5th, 1999, sadly i know the date)
not knowing Eliza was getting off too
            and soon to be getting off again

i watched them walk out together
        knowing what was up
she had told me recently that she
        was over him
        but fuck did she lie

thinking they were in her or his car
        munching away on each others' members
Kris started on the ski simulator game
        and Eliza pulled me aside
a few months back she had told me
        that she had woken up
        with the intention of losing her virginity
shit, i've woken up like that
        a thousand times
but being a guy
        it's a lot harder
        to cash that in

anyway
        she told me that her friend
        & her friend's parents were out of town
and she had a key to use their house
        for a special purpose
yet the night she first told me this
        she didn't utilize it
so she laid this on me again
        knowing exactly what it meant
not only does she have
        the fucking nerve to come and tell me
        she is going to fuck Kris
not just fuck him,
        but give her virginity to him
she asks me for
        a fucking condom!
you know i'm no baby
        who would bitch about petty shit
it's not jealousy that pissed me off
        but the fact that she knew
        what she meant to me
and it's as if she didn't care
        about my feelings
her friend

        a person whom trusts her
her friend
        a person whom loves her
her friend

things were different from then on
we were never the same

but

not even a month later
        we fucked for three hours

                                    [previously unreleased]

virgin nature

autumn leaves breath life
where coital pleasures can't intrude
spring breezes bend steel currents
an orgasm of purity, fellatio can't top
summer heat, melts tarry roofs
a temperature cunnilingus won't produce
winter chills cut through glass
forever beginning the cycle

and the sex of virgin nature

non-repeated repetition

transponding thoughts of sea-foam skin
an unearthly dream of psychedelic creations
i want to feel no pain
little boys, in creeks, finding adventure
growing strong, turning grey, staying young
judge me no more
no longer prostitute my love
in the land of ivory bullets
       with chromium shells
       dipped in rotten flesh
judge me
i want to feel

dogmatic flaws

tiger stripes cross leopard spots
     in the zoo inside myself
delving deeper into crevices not known
claws extract, pierce and cling
scratching the flesh
     beckoning blood
make me smile
     masochist dreams with sadist attire
ethical boundaries stepped upon and over
i care no more
     morals infallible
break down the genes of human animals
split the atom of my earthly form
     in the zoo inside myself
slits overtake my eyes
tigers stride dominantly
crossing leopard spots
make me smile

the plunge

stares out the window
seeing the world
     its beauty
its immortality
     its never-ending cycle
between me and this beauty
     a layer of glass
thin   fragile   man-made
holding me back
     teasing my senses
there is more out there than what i can see
more beauty?   yes
darker things too

burnt tenements
flesh-molded alleys
     cum-covered walls

     intercourse in a syringe

unknown random writing   4

i'm sitting on "the bridge" at my school writing
upon a bench, next to a window, sun belting in
there is a retarded boy named Jake
        a few benches down
i don't like laughing at them
        or making fun of them
but sometimes you can't help it
i feel sorry for them sometimes
they may never experience love or sex or anything
but then i think that they won't know
        they are missing anything
i'm content with that
        i guess

                                    [previously unreleased]

unknown random writing   5

today i read Jim Carroll's Void of Course
        and jim morrison's The Lord and the New Creatures
two books in one day
fucking crazy
i used to hate reading
i'm going to start here soon a book of poems
        by robert frost

it's as if i have become a poet and a diarist myself
and strangely i have
i am a poet
quoting myself a few years ago
        "poetry's fucking gay"

now, my friends,
        it has become my salvation

                                    [previously unreleased]

dead alive

colored blackness drifts apart
as it closes in
a drowning barracuda dives deeper
causing a falling albatross to soar
blind eyes watch me
fixated on my opaquely translucent skin
covered in sweat my dry skin cracks
reaching up to touch the ground
      i fall to the sky

stop the rain

encrusted tombs of ancient rites
stand tall, like babel
      to the heavens above
a bell rings, i hear
      it shatters my vision

limestone carvings, beautiful at a glance,
      worn away after decades
a lively boy sits, wearing thin, growing old
dying, slowly
the world tries to kill him
      from inside out
      outside in

blazing stars shine eloquently and bright
watching them we watch a death
dying and dead stars are gazed upon
stars we see are already dead
a lively boy sits
      already dead

_____ **no difference**

sensually silky smooth,
　　　blessed be those who massage others
rough and dry, a working man's nature
　　　puts food on the table
the power to crash and caress
to scratch and bruise
　　　to stroke and pat
they can sit and rest like tigers in tall grass
may be fast and furious
　　　if orchestrating a harmonious concerto
moving swift and briskly
　　　scribbling down bits of words
　　　code, feelings, soul

hidden beneath a texture layer is the ability to kill
　　　rape　　maim
those choices share seats
　　　with love　　　save　　help
we have not only one kind
　　　but all

the sky is the limit
and yet it is not
reaching above the sky you find heaven
and from heaven you derive what choices to make

kill　　save
rape　　love
maim　　help

the blood of christ may be on them
did you hurt or help?

ash lakes

emerald stars
in a ruby sky

diamond dandelions sway
swiftly in opal grass

children play   prismatic   unending
amethyst pupils

studded nerves bear winged stripes
carving crevices in their hearts
like glaciers in a burnt-sienna mountain

here i soar, flying high
as a leper eagle

here, i descend
parts of me falling
            faster than i

        in a ruby sky

torment and pain *

as i looked into the eyes of god
i saw myself
            a reflection from his divine eyes
i did not like who i saw
i saw a weak man
i saw a prick
i saw ...

a martyr

gravity

a dark horseman rides the crimson dusk
until night overpowers and shows its fascist head
dripping fangs tainted with virgin blood
albino eyes with ash-white face
stare up
      crying, regretting
the sins of the past strike forth
a violent blow, a barbaric force
repenting their sins is not an option
no time left for them

a sword rises high, blocking the creamy moon
with one swipe
      the disease called "sinners" is wiped out
the horseman retreats to the seventh layer
small drops leave a trail behind
from these drops grow trees of deceit and pain
trees to feed future sinners
apples blossom
      the sun peeks out

      as new blood slithers past

linklater was right
darkness brings many things in this place
beatings, numerous rapes
narcotic gangs are in power
in cohorts with alcoholic cliques
torture is an everyday occurrence

this is where i live
in this place of bias and consumerism
this is the suburbs

people think that violence and hatred
      is limited to the inner city.
shit, i wish. i've lived in the 'burbs all my life
      and i see no difference in any actions
      just difference in perspectives
if the 'burbs are such a sanctuary
      then why do i hurt so?
      and i'm not alone
it is, however, my black hell

do come in

————————————

this ain't no Tom Hanks film
      or 'American Beauty'
even though 'American Beauty'
      is the closest representation i've seen
it's not 'My Blue Heaven'
      Steve Martin is not around
it is, however, my black hell

do come in

[second part - previously unreleased]

it's funny how unexpected things happen
actually it's quite sad
it is also interesting how a day can start off one way
       and end up completely different
my girlfriend Marilyn and i came back to my house
       about 1 a.m.
my parents were home
       but that didn't matter
she didn't have to be home
       'til 3 a.m. because her parents
       thought she was at a cast party
for the play she starred in that night
       'the chalk garden'

as soon as we got into my room
       we undressed & made the sweetest
       and greatest love of all time
it was different than any other time
it was slow and sweet and more orgasmic
       than anytime before

flash forward
       fourteen hours

she came over later
       and as soon as i saw her
       i knew something was different
i said nothing

Kirk was there too
but after awhile
       it was just her and i

we were lying on my futon
i was almost falling asleep when she got up
       and started to leave
i asked her where she was going
she said she didn't know
she stood at the doorway
       watching me for about five minutes
then she walked off
inside me i kept thinking

"get up"
"go after her"
but there i sat

twenty minutes passed
        and she came back upstairs
        and sat beside me
by this time a thousand things
        had gone through my mind
thinking she wanted to leave me
wondering if i should leave her
we sat for ten minutes before i asked
        "what is this?"
referring to the situation
she said she didn't know
that's all i want to say for now

----

we broke up
due to my actions
i thought that i wasn't ready
        and needed some time
she ran off crying
        and at that moment i realized
        what a mistake i had made
i cried in the bathroom
        for about twenty minutes
then i sat for another ten
        staring at my empty fish tank
all i thought about was how to get her back

i felt i needed to get out so i went
        to my friend Will's house
we were loading a tank into the back of my truck
when i told him that we had broken up
he said nothing verbally
as i looked at him
        his eyes said everything
his reaction was as if what i said
        was more surprising than if i told him
        i killed his parents
Will also helped me realize

what i did was wrong
i didn't plan on telling
        Kirk quite yet
and Will wouldn't say anything
however Kirk figured it out anyway
he could tell by my voice
        and how Marilyn and i
        were acting earlier

i went home and called her cell phone
        and left four messages
        saying that i was sorry
        and that i needed to talk to her
she called me back at ten
        and luckily she took me back

i finally realized what i wanted
        and she was it

                        [previously unreleased]

doorway of glory

closing my eyes i feel all
i see all and all sees me
imagining a crystal lake
      calm as a mirror
      motionless
my foot steps upon it
the skin is tickled by its coldness
it's solid and cold
      yet not ice

my heart loosens
all things bred of hate
      leave from within
high above
a sky almost cloudless
there is
      however
one lone cloud
i gaze upon it
      as i take its shape
      and place
floating high above the mirror lake
      cold and crystal
i am now floating vapor
      but feel solid
the gates open

i am finally accepted

redeemed

serene beauty of enormous proportions
flaws of the eye
felt, not seen
take me back
        back to my life

my sanctuary of love

doves cry no more

lusting eyes float upon turquoise waves
a gliding waltz of coital pleasure
each step taken seals minor cracks
sea spray excites the senses
an orgasmic rush overthrows
salty foam trickles down her smooth creamy skin
her slender fingers run up my chest and over my chin
to gracefully stroke anxiously awaiting lips
lips finally touch as a cold sensation runs down our spines
lightning strikes from her heart to mine
our chemistry creates a small ecosystem between us
rainy mists spray within
emotions spoken
        not by words
        but by love's precipitation

forecast calls for a bright sunny life
with a hundred percent chance of eternal love

weak man's exit

my taste buds are slightly excited as the metal enters my mouth. the blue cobalt steel makes teeth chatter with its coldness, salivary glands overflow making up for the acidic effect of the bitter taste. a large spiked ball resides in my chest, blocking air and causing pain. the ball is pain, and torment. long dirty hair hangs over my face covering up the hands holding the steel. a steady shaking overtakes my head, a small cramp swells in my neck. moisture collects in the corner of my eye, rushing over that sleep dust which still sits from yesterday. too tired to wipe clear. a small drop falls from my eye and catches a foothold on my cheek, running slowly, ever so slowly down to my quivering guilt-stricken lips. it continues, over the lips and onto the steel. its watery texture gradually turns from shape to shape, adjoining and contorting, collaborating with every minute crease and particle on the blue cobalt.

upon reaching the line between steel and walnut it pauses, i gaze at it as it sits, taking in a deep inhalation. for a split second my mind is clear, i think to myself, "why am i doing this?" before i answer, however, the whistle is blown, break time is over, the drop continues. driving faster now, for the walnut has a waterproof finish. the liquid once again touches metal, cobalt blue. it consumes, the liquid that is, letters etched in the polished blue, metal, cobalt. as it continues it deforms the letters, a section at a time. 'winchester' is contorted to many different likenesses. and then it happens, the cold liquid makes its final descent to my trembling finger, resting on the trigger of cobalt blue.

opus of a mad jack

my opus. i don't believe that it is my job to prepare my own opus, at least not literally. it can't be something i create from my own mind. not a collection of poems, a diary, a novel or a film. what i leave behind can not be something that i put forth with the intent of people noticing. that is not me. no matter what you do, if you do it so someone else sees it you put on this false façade to try and be better or look cooler. in my poetry i use metaphors and symbolism to describe how i see the world, in my journal i write about how the world affects me, and in the screenplays that i scribe i try and pawn off all of my troubles and torment onto a fictitious character, trying to remove my problems while also venting anger. these actual works can never be my true opus. but how people perceive them can. in a film i write it may not be the dialogue that a character says, but the meaning and the power that came from me to write that dialogue. in my poetry it is not the words i want to stick in peoples' minds, but the images and the emotions that the words create.

my opus isn't just something that i can write, but actual feelings i display to the world. if it is merely opening a door for a young lady, or telling a lovely lady that she has pretty hair, and changing the course of her day. my opus is not only how my work may change people but how i am remembered and how i changed peoples' lives.

i've never been the greatest man, i have tried but i always fuck things up. i've cheated on people, teased people for no reason, treated people like shit because i thought that i was better than them. which of course is far from the truth. my opus is whatever people will remember about me. whether it is good or bad. i will be content with either. if you remember me as an arrogant prick, so be it, and if you think i am the sweetest guy in the world, cool. i have you fooled, but cool. i just want to be remembered.

gestation

as the hourglass fills, my heart spills
to the floor, i'm out of time
trying to recall what i did or didn't do
why does it matter?
      i'm sorry what i did to you

your innocent smile and lusting eyes
not seeing i'm your devil in disguise

the bond remains, love fills my veins
too bad we're out of time

your juices flow as my lips touch yours
our skin is moist and legs entwined

i am inside you although i hurt you
      how are you still able to moan?

the feeling back then was one of trust
now that is all but lost
my love flows, from me to you
to create a love for both
time marches on
      the love is born
i'm sorry i left you alone

psychodynamica

i scream inside
    at night alone
the pains crescendos, my hope dies down
voices fill my melancholy head
they whisper things evil and true
        things i dread
if i'm but one, who would care?
i'm on my own filled with despair
i cast out dreams, wishes and ambitions
why do they matter?
god? if you are real can you hear me?
        can you help me?

help me fight, stop the rage
        give me hope?
if i gave up all my problems would cease
        and i'd be free
        free

i am free in truth, no one holds me back
people do back me
        yet
i'm a freak on a leash with a grip on myself
i feel trapped by visions, things from the past
        good and bad
i envision things i don't need
        but want and will never have
it is like i am a pain junkie
        and i get off on my own torment

at night alone
        i scream inside

solar paradise

virgin isles with sandy beaches
a young lover, starfish eyes
lying naked on smooth white sand
shuffling the body sends orgasmic rushes
        from head to toe
soft summer breezes, caress the hairs
flowing like grass
a cloud blocks the sun's path
covering the lover in shadows
chills overrunning the rushes of orgasmic sand
a gentle rain follows
washing away the heat, washing away the pleasure
the lover retreats to his room
fire ignites, sheets cover
a new sun shines
the smile of his lover
her hands touch his body
flowing like grass
the sex of summer begins

on an isle with sandy beaches

_____ **self-titled**

rain drops of eerie precision
run down my back
wearing away the layers of sanctity
leaving a canyon of hurt
into these voids is a secretion
a falsity to bide the time
'til it all wears away
helping all but feel alone
each drop of moisture
erases a coveted memory
      a time of joy and purity
      innocence   and love

      being free and young
      awaiting it all

the calm before the storm
      playing   not knowing
      playing   yeah   playing

i was a child then ...

into the void

serious thoughts awaken
my angelically sleeping head
dreams of sex and masturbatory wishes
vanish
       bye bye

hello new concerns of trivial feces
stuff that doesn't matter but makes me rage
this struggle takes its toll after time
eroding my already bruised soul
       bye bye

putrid soldiers of material things
invade my narrow mind
my ass don't need this
don't deserve this
don't need this
fuck it all away
       bye bye

_____ **hellbound**

terror reaffirms its place
wreaking havoc on us sinners
causing us to kill
        although it is fun

a man draws in a breath
a breath exhaled by god
the man dies
carbon dioxide kills

if god had shared his breath
the man would have lived
but god doesn't share
the sadist fuck

try lending a hand
        we do

learn from us
try for once
        we do

gauged

the taste of blue cobalt steel
in your mouth is good
except when there is a trigger
at the other end
      one slip, no more
      one slip, good-bye

have you ever watched a tear slowly fall?
from your eye to your nose
from your nose to your lip
to the long barrel of blue steel
      traveling
      traveling
'til it hits the walnut stock
and runs across your trembling finger

      one slip

bosch barracuda

dreams of tomorrow break
inside my congealed head
taking in   absorbing
my taste buds are excited
      by grit and steel
      the two minerals of a content life form
salty like tear drops
acidic like lime
eyelids droop
      as i become erect

crying an orgasm of tears
sulfuric stench of sex
slimy wax of ear-like form
sliding down my drums

playing a pizzicato suite
i slowly tap my foot to the beat

into your eyes

bleeding my soul
a tortured diary, spurts forth
covering canvas with maroon encryptions
a macabre of idealism and sorrow
surrealism overpowers
a poetic playground
        romantic swings
        mystic jungle
a complex chutes and ladders
        slide forth
        blood lubricating walls
creaking of steel on steel
breaking of a childhood mindset

the beginning descent
        clothed in striped socks knee high
        halfway, jeans and a tee
"this is the end," morrison said
clothed in wrinkles and a three piece
hush puppy feet
        silence sights, seen over ages
blood puppies adorn my soul and soles
covered in my tortured diary
        maroon encryptions
things long ago seem real, too real
things long ago are real, too real

my soul bleeds
down my white tee, streaking my striped socks
covering my hush puppy feet
        in this poetic   romantic
        mystic jungle

puma

a ladder of sixty-eight
upon four i stand
glaring up
seeing the worn soles of others before me
ascending to righteousness
       struggle
       struggle
make it to five
my muscles contract
pulling so hard
bleeding inside
i feel the flow
at thirty seven there is a rest stop
a constant raining of urine
soaks me
make it to five
who tied my laces to the rung?
they prevent my success
       yet i'm bare foot

see hear speak think

starting in the realm of loneliness
i follow the blazing star
to the land of hope
       a sea port
harboring brothers
the four stand together
       as one
all following the same path
to meet this day
a glorious day
when the sky turned from gray
we stood tall
fighting them all
preventing the fall
       of another
gripping tight
       the hands of our brother

_____ **yellow prick road**

on my journey towards insanity
i stop to smell the briar patch
for a briar by any other name
            would smell as sweet
it cuts my nose

avoiding a patch of roses
for fear they might scratch
others follow, i lead the way
my eyes
            body
            and soul
all monochromatic gray
staring into an abyss
            it also sees me
i toss in a nickel
willie and the poor boys don't take pennies
spotted zebras pounce the striped dalmatian

i touch myself, no one sees
polka dot bandana strangles my conceited skull
blood backs up
pressure builds
wondering what size shoe that snake wears
wait, they don't have feet
maybe he'll prefer sandals
shedding away inhibitions

the abyss also sees me

to alex*

in a numerical system of love
17 and 18 have the ability
        to make 1
combining of dual 23's
        makes 1
the adding of an extra
        creates a strange one

if told i was to be a father i'd choke
my heart would stop
and my heart would cease
not from shock mind you
nor horror
thoughts would overload
my butter-like cerebral processor
all choices at said point in time would equal
the sum of "shit!"
        a small percentage "shit, yes!"
        a small percentage "shit, we can't afford it."
and a disturbing percentage
        "shit, my child must die."

the changeling

a freight train glides drably
careening over perpendicular steel and wood
imbedded spikes stab my scaly foot
tiptoe through the garden
of bubonic decay and pornographic waste
a picture of me is covered in feces
celestial rays pivot and swirl about
a psycho disco full as a reservoir
        preserving liquid asphalt
        to solidify and crash
rusted frames surrounding images
born of my creativity and lust
the train collides with insanity
instead of giving it a lift

last in line

no poem can ever suffice
      ever explain
      ever end
the feelings and thoughts inside my head
i write and write and the worse i feel

if i stop i'll fill up with hate and anger
i realized, finally
      that i am evil
      not divine

everyone hurts, all i care about is me
hurting others to fulfill my needs
the antichrist has been born
inside my mind, inside my body
      killing my soul
sometimes things that should affect me
      aren't even noticed
they are dealt away like deuces
      no matter the hand
i'll bet it all
      no matter their bet
all their worth
i'll take it, exploit it and laugh
      i am evil
      not divine

_____ **i don't exist**

sometimes i think
while i lie here awake
why has god done this to me?

i tried to be good
but folks never would
open their hearts and give in

i wish sometimes
that i was someone else
then maybe i'd finally win

rage fills my mind
as it eats me inside
why must it always be me?

please, please let me in
i know i can be someone better
nothing matters to me anymore
just wanting to see what god has in store

why why can't i be free?
        free
i know i am evil
but give me a chance
i serenade with the devil
        a sorrowful dance

__inner fury__

tilling a river of my creations
fording a flowing delta of emotions
rushing forth
a damnation to the lower realm
inviting my distempered soul
dogma destroyed by realism
creationism thrown out by facts of evolution
capitalism fueled by corruption
burning strong, glowing bright
ephemeral images glorified like saints
standing high above peasants
royalty still rules
the faces of martyrs flash forward
preaching the power of the almighty
miracles performed by gentiles
blasted forth, ascending the social pyramid
virgin goddesses bearing fruit
flowering like a spring bud
blossoming infidelity
coveting the mate of another
young boys break the soul
reaching out, becoming men
rebirth through the dying of innocence

repercussions

blowing ever so lovely i watch her shining hair
its beauty is not just its appearance
for there is more to it
and more to her
her eyes tell me that she hurts
has always been hurt
yet hopefully will never be hurt again
it's assumed that she has enemies
and has been labeled profanely
these labels are not her all the time
just on occasions, when she can no longer hold back
it is sad that such lovely people are slowly ate away
by incompetent others who
having no self-esteem themselves,
find their salvation by ruining others

have you ever watched a leaf
            stuck in a blade of grass?
it struggles to be free, and show its independence
the wind is a soft voice telling it to "go"
and gently gives it a push
the grass, sadly, becomes the antagonist
holding back the leaf
holding back its hope, holding its soul
            and preventing its freedom

change your view for a moment
the grass is a mother-being, using maternal instincts
to preserve the leaf's sanctity
what if the wind was a foe?
telling the leaf to go for it, be free, and fight the power
but what can the wind offer?
no set destination, no secure place to fall
just a wild ride through the sky with no boundaries

the leaf i watched is now gone

a legacy of rage
a farewell to Brandon Lee

too early your star burnt out
a light taken from our eyes
you burned so fast and bright
taken, one unfortunate night

in your wake you stunned millions
with your beauty
            brilliance
            strength
i knew you not, but i knew you well
your smiling face forever etched in my mind

we loved you Brandon, always will
you watch down over us now
forever we gaze up to see your shining light
it burnt out, but believers still see

more than an actor or martial artist you were
but a friend and idol
we were lucky to have seen you
in your blaze of glory

your name forever on our lips
part of you embedded in our souls
guiding us in ways unimaginable
we love you
            jesus wept for you my friend

clock dog

days keep spinning fearlessly
time advances knowing no boundaries
still not knowing where to head
which door shall i open?
which pill shall i take?
shall i grow taller?
or shrink smaller?
click my heels, return home?
follow the red brick road?
or the one less traveled by?
a prepared fate
made of silver not clay
worth much
but not malleable
not changeable
forever fixed

my wheel in the sky keeps on turning

diamond

through the tempered glass window
a pedophile old man creeps slowly
over the fence, through the bushes and trees
into the shed
my eyes glued to it
walking forward opening the tempered glass
crawling through, pant cuff tugging
eyes never leaving the pedophile shed
i walk slowly but swiftly to the steel construction

entering the abode my eyes were fixed upon
        empty, no man

           no creeping man
           no pedophile creeping man
           old man creeping pedophile   no

knees shake as my hair blows
like dust in the wind

turn my back still feeling a presence
the man has invaded me
he's not here now
        but will always be there creeping
an unconscious part always knowing
i was fooled, i was beaten
the man overtook me
crept into the shed
        of my mind

life accumulus

some days i'm slow, hardly move
not noticeable
movement not seen unless
not focused upon

focus on object stationary
blurrily see me move

some days i'm fast
blowing hard, cycloning around grayish
not keeping up
       forever moving, forever changing
totally different now than i was
       ten minutes ago
       ten minutes from now

different than now
swirling, cycloning, spinning
changing forms
       forever moving

some days i'm not even here

tripsy

for Marilyn•

she doesn't see good looks
she doesn't see wealth
    whether i have either

she doesn't see popularity
she doesn't see talent
    whether i have either

i ask myself
"if she doesn't see me for those things, what does she see in me?"

she sees me
    the one who holds her close
    the one who writes her poems
    the one who strokes her silky hair
    the one who sings to her

she sees me
    the one who completes her

quoting Harry Chapin
    "may i some day be what it is she sees in me."

it's always tuesday at my house

for Will •

12 years ago i met you
softball brought us together
never crossing my mind
          that you would be there forever
it's amazing how two people
totally different, are so alike
both driven to lenexa
to build a friendship, a bond
a bond that never breaks
          never fades, never will
i never told you "i love you"
do i even need to?
i'm sure you know
looking at you i don't see "my friend Will."
i see another part of me
hobbies and passions are different
but we learn from one another
i feel so secure around you
you'll never judge me, never turn on me
          never rub my mistakes in my face
it's great how i don't need to ask you to keep a secret
it would be an insult if i did
even though you are so talented it makes me sick
i'll still put up with you
          master carpenter, mechanic
          guitarist, pool shark
          artist, friend
i've learned so much from you Will
mainly how much love two men can share
i've just one question
are you scared of the future too?
will it always be the four of us?
i'm sure we'll be together
me and my brother who speaks no evil

'cuda been better

for Kirk •

out of everyone i know
you are the most cherished to me
we are so alike it boggles my mind
we've both seen things and felt things
        we wish to forget
we struggle through our art
        to release the pain from within
i look at you sometimes
        and i know what you are thinking
        that alone scares me
you have thought things that aren't right
i won't ignore the fact that you aren't always happy
but you know i'm here
you are more like a brother than almost anyone
do you feel the same way?
you'll always have a place in my heart
when you hurt i do the same
if you cried so did i
the glory and power you harbor is so amazing
the artwork you love, but pretend not to
the common knowledge
        you are too bright
        for your own good sometimes
the humor you have
        i can't look at you without smiling
it's etched in my mind that you will always strive on
be strong i know you can
the road ahead is bumpy and unsure
fight it, i'll be here to help
i love you more than life itself
i'm sure we'll be together
me and my brother who hears no evil

the song remains the same*

for Tim

it is funny how even years later
             i still see you as the new guy
you've been with us for seven long years
and you still have this freshness
you must admit that you haven't always followed
             the same path as me and the others
veering off the road many times
             in many ways
other friends you have made may help you
             procure your chemical needs
but can they offer the trust and love that we can?
it's highly unimaginable
you and i have been through a lot
seeing and doing things just plain crazy
but we still play on
i do still have a feeling that there is
             a secret battle waiting in the wings
a final confrontation
one more decision to make
it is possible we lose you to chemical needs
but we both know we can win
you don't know how much you mean to me as a friend
losing you is one thing
             losing you to a chemical is another
our future sucks us closer everyday
our lives will change in dramatic ways
i'm sure we'll be together
me and my brother who thinks no evil

sixpence all the richer

for Caroline •

as friends go
my eyes have been opened by you more than anyone
although as a girlfriend
        it was a struggle to win your heart
but as a friend you slid into my arms
i'd always known
there was more to a relationship than sex
not until you did i experience love
love that was so pure
sex wasn't needed to hold it together
while even though
        you have almost gone from my life
the memories, feelings and lessons
        i got from you live on
you meant a lot to me
just thought you should know

this will not do

writing on a fresh blank page seems so obscure
it becomes a game, with no winners
it is like ruining something pure
marking on its cleanliness
how much is enough to write to justify your writing?
is five lines a waste of paper?
is fifty lines cramming too much on one page?
parts of thoughts can never be erased
secret enemies aspire through creativity
slowly gyrating
pulling your atoms like strings
a puppet you are to these invisible hands
in your head
your oily hand shuffling across the plain white
jade fingerprints not viewable by your ruby eyes
shafts of light melting the nickel from your name
       onto your silver tongue
maniacal forces driving semis of rage
through the highways of your ear canals
screaming loudly eastbound and down
smoking like the bandit

you know shit

kansas is home to more than fields of wheat,
       flying houses and munchkins
the county in which i live is one of the richest
and most prosperous
in the world
it shows, which makes me sick
       we sit, supposedly in a dream world
       we sit, not knowing how the world works
       we sit, so naive and innocent
       we sit, born with silver spoons
       and high allowances
       we sit, not seeing the pain others experience
if you think this who the fuck are you to judge?
if we're so rich why do we hurt so bad?
money can't buy happiness everyone knows that
if we don't know how the world works
       how can we learn
if teens are labeled as evil and have a stigma
       placed on them
       and are so naive and innocent
why do we help make more changes
       in society than adults?
all you see in us is rap and hard rock music
       teenage alcoholics and youthful sex fiends
       druggies and jocks
       freaks and preps
kids who shoot up schools for no reason
sadly we have reasons for lashes of violence
to revolt against the government
       for not regulating the media
the media runs us all
       never showing teenage glory
       just teenage guts
we never do anything good
       except conjure up news-worthy events

chamber

in the woods i find a sense of freedom
the smell of crystal leaves with pine tar wood
fear is left in the anal sex of the city
its rottenness and filth, its unclean purity
walking through the woods as tall as mountains
i venture back to adolescence
cool blowing breezes
      the chill of rain
standing naked i feel secure
the forest clothes me
its million-mile-high canopy
      blocks out harsh demonic storms
fallen bark covers me
termites tickle my nerves
i kind of like it
a warmth continuous throughout my body
even in a wintery snow
i run free, arms outstretched
like razors, cutting down my forest
exposing me for what i am
an insecure boy, naked in the forest
drenched in april showers
heading back to be raped by the city

the end of innocence *

i remember when i was young
watching 'Heathcliff', 'Thundercats', and 'Voltron'
running through backyards
        shooting fake guns
arguing over who shot who first
carrying around a plastic whiffle ball bat
thinking i was Luke skywalker
Nintendo was fun, i loved 'Duck Hunt'
except for that damned laughing dog
'The Goonies', 'The Lost Boys', 'The Breakfast Club'
films of my generation that will always
        'Stand By Me'
i remember when i was young
a time before the back yards were fenced
a time of purity and joy
        innocence and love
        being young and free
        awaiting it all
the calm before the storm
        playing, not knowing
        playing, yeah, playing
i was a child then ...

time

around me the leaves are still
      the trees don't sway
sun beating down
      no breeze today
a tyrannical wind blows
      and tears through the chamber of my mind
      it hurts, it does
too many questions
too many thoughts
      goals, dreams, hopes
none to focus on
life spins around me, me standing still
clouds fade off leaving me bare
material things are all i strive for
it's such a fucking waste
ten years from now i will have everything
everything i wanted that is
yet inside i will still be a child
wanting nothing but more ...

altercation

the face in the mirror
why does it have to be mine?
i see my own image corrupt and evil
hoping to see the image of old
ten years back
the image of who i was
ten years back
the image of who i am not anymore

dark child

he wipes the blood from his ashen hands
a melancholy burden of pure hatred
dark shots of cynic juice
invades his veins overturning
overtaking, burning
the eyes raise and they slowly burn
glowing red and ferocious, fiery
they melt his heart into a pool

he dives in and is swallowed
by a satanic creation
born of love

requiem for a martyr

its slimy skin engulfs my soul
        wrapping, sliding
        feeling, grinning
slowly fueling the rage
awaiting a pernicious end
it will never die, i know this
i shall never quit
i'll fight and tear and punch and kick
through bile and blood and piss and shit
the lake of fire will never be home
it will never be my master
its lair is not as safe as thought
its overconfidence will be its downfall
paradise was once lost and then regained
i know i can do the same

it slithers and slithers, forth and back
it does not own me, but believes it so
what force is biding its time?
i know not, but am curious to know
the end is near
        for i have foreseen
sadistically glad this is no dream
my position in hell i hold it firm
the lake of fire my palace
my brother the worm

white heat

there will always be two doors
to any house
anywhere
in and out
out and in
front and back
back and front
choices there will always be
right and wrong
wrong and right
dreams in the day
dreams at night
behind each door is a path
an in, back and right
or
an out, front, and wrong
choose wisely your door
especially if you live
on the edge

so mote it be

powers of the dark compel me
to do what needs to be done
i take a stand for my cause
protect it
i pray you sinners to run
no attention will be paid to race, sex, or class
the end is drawing near
i'll watch and wait
the day it comes to pass
i am the son of my father
and a leader he is to me
after we destroy you
we can be free
the dark angel, the worm and me

chelsea remembered
remembered the first "i love you"
      that came from his mouth
it meant a lot to her
to him it was just words
words to keep her mind busy
he had just had his fingers
      in her snatch
and it was the first time
      he had ever touched one
he had dreamed about it
curious as to what it
      would feel like
      and smell like
he now knew both
he was curious
      about the taste
      but didn't press his luck
the words "i love you" he thought
      would stick in her mind
make her think that he
      liked her for her
not just because he could
      cop a feel of her crotch
the words meant a lot to her
she felt comforted by them
even though she could
      feel the lie

[previously unreleased]

the unicorn

it stood in the sun after a day of rain
the smell of the rain overpowering
but not as much as its beauty
the graceful movements and sparkling eyes
so amazed i was, to see one as fine
i strive to attain and take control
my actions premature
creeping over to catch it i always made a noise
snapped a twig, popped a joint
it always retreated, moved away
leaving me in its wake, in its fresh prints
i wanted it to be mine
so badly i did but never got close
            then i finally realized
maybe it's not scared of me, my actions
            or my intentions
it doesn't mind me looking or wanting
as long as that's all
it just wants to be left alone
control its own life, makes its own path
it's not that it didn't want anyone approaching
            it just didn't want me
on first realization that hurt, but the hurt faded away
i now feel privileged to have known it
to have seen it, in its innocence
and to have been able to watch it grow and change
be molded to what it is today
not better or worse, just different
people always say you can't catch a unicorn
and that they do not exist
they do exist, we just picture them wrong
and you can catch a unicorn
just not your unicorn
your unicorn is that one girl
the one who will always get away

_____tral
for Hubert

Selby dreamed the dream of a chilling requiem
giving beauty to pain and pain to beauty
taking the exit of the last to brooklyn and its past
showing us real life
helping us understand what it takes to be free
we all grow and die like a weeping willow tree
we all have our demons to be killed and cast aside
it is not easy, never think it so
you'll truly be surprised
inside we see things made up or real
remember the way we want
not exactly how it happened
thinking about those times in your room
      when trapped by your mind
sing daily, sing nightly
sing it soft and slow
sing of your dream of your demon
your exit or your room
or the places you wish to go
sing with your willow tree
the song of the silent snow

legend

there is a shocking legend
        of halsey and 51st
quarrels never cease of which version is the worst
a story of coincidence
        a matter of fact
        and chance
details so minute
almost choreographed like a dance
evidence exists that proves the story true
it happened on a cold dark night
it's as real as me and you
quarrels never cease
debates never end
of which version is pure truth
and the best to defend
this is the shocking legend
        of halsey and 51st
have a gander be prepared
this version is the worst

biddy diddy bop
(a bop diddy biddy)

ozark mountains, plains,
      rivers, trees
a virgin boy, blond hair shorn
young jezebel, on her knees
the breeze is cool, the water chills
trickles of sensation, and myriad thrills
black heart dialectic cliques
denim neo-nazi hippie chicks
cinematic pedophiles with fecal fetish
long-haired hip cat
      with a high-strung pernicious wish
cum-stained boxers on a pubic-free ball
look at the sky, wanting to fall
iraqi camel-fucker, horse-licker, cock-shit
young snatch with peanut butter gyrating cat's nip
programmed junkies with remote controlled veins
digital pyros, heroin at the reins
emerald quarry like the city of oz
corrupting a virgin or someone who never was
display the patriarchs and patricide
fast forward through the anarchists and genocide
scribing a requiem of mortal abortions
fetal deaths make up the mass
eat the fucker that choked the class
shoot up the venom of blood-crazed lesbos
with acid-washed skin on rock-hard tiptoes
Smith said "kiss me good-bye"
      and watched, "the animals die."
Carroll wrote," little kids shoot marbles
      where branches break the sun ..."
Kerouac, Ginsberg and Cassady paved the way
      for the asphalt revolution
P.T. bore a new age genre with style
      and truth and balls
watching dirk diggler rise
      and the exodus frogs fall

________ **cock**

we are not children
we are not youth
we are not nice, so fuck you
we are strong
we are powerful, so fuck you
we do not like you
we do not want you
we do not respect you, so fuck you
we do hate you
we do fuck you
we do own you, so fuck you
we do not love you
we do not need you
we want to fucking kill you
we run this fucking country
we run this fucking world
we know there is nothing you can do
        so fuck you
we will fucking rape you as you did us
corrupt you as you did us
        so fuck you

bourgeoisie

i

people spend their days
spinning like a top
a bunch of mindless fucking sheep
i wish it'd fucking stop

ii

a woman touched my heart
before it was fully grown
like a butterfly
with molested wings
i could never fly again

iii

i can feel the tension mounting
building like a volcano
on the verge of orgasm
what a poor pathetic soul i am
not fit for any love
you laugh at me and so do i
who gives a flying fuck?

iv

there is a place
i see it in my dreams
i see this face, pale
in this place, and it screams
it echoes and resonates
reverberates and dies
the torment is seen
in its dark bloody eyes

turn

fearing the night
is sum-thing eyve dun
has'ent every 1 dun it 2
oar am i aloan agin?
at tymes i can sea clearlee
mostly it is blurred
i serch in the knight
four a purpuss   a wurd
but nuthin i've fownd
never ceesus two ah-maize-mee
how dum i can feel
spinning iz my mynd
on a nevur terning wheel

paradice lust

cumming n2 the glorie daze
i slowlee fade aweigh
feeling the death march closing n
their requiem startz to play
the con-duck-tore in the black vale
raises his baton and taps his toe
scrap-en the assphalt (fault) with his spur
lowers the brim of his cow-boy hat
and blinks his skull-e i

jubilaytion nites

once i had this dream
where eye dyed in a pool of pure hate
coal-ectd o'er years and yeers
hate that poored out of my brow
like a black viscous sweat
dipped my finger n it eye did
raysed it 2 my lips
tasted it bitter   ver-e bitter
butt boy wuz it grate

cervasa

if you look closely at a stick of gum
you can see the face of god
i noticed that one day when eating cheetos

ever since then i've been different
i've felt this overpowering presence
like a friend or helping hand

i no longer feel alone
that's all i've ever wanted ...

      he looked like a flavor crystal

quasar rhyts

rolling waves crash in my mind
eroding the dreams of childhood
there are these misfit sinners
sinners in my mind, in my head
in my soul, burrowing
      and killing me
slowly and surely
for centuries they have striven
ancient mysteries were born
through their power
      (jesus why do i hurt?)
through their will
i must conquer them
kill them
mass genocide is in my eyes

drug regime

bands strike up
and it hurts me
it feels like a thousand knives
i hate the way it makes me feel
   both half dead
   half alive
the only thing
that makes me strive on
is a dying want to not
shit pisses me off
especially when it is not shit
but something that is
but ain't also
and something
that never won't be
what it is not

  it makes sense to me

6n8t7

51st i see it
like it was that day
standing beside Carroll, diary in hand
we talked and played and talked and regaled
Carroll and i, the diary, the field
he talked of the past, things he'd seen
i spoke of the future, my hopes and dreams
our generations contrast
our styles the same
one thing that's not different is the people we blame
for deaths, for rapes
for pain, for hate
for lying, for cheating
for saying it's too late
      our parents, our teachers
      our policeman, our priests
      our elders, our bosses
our socially-distorted, unfaithful doubting beasts
unlike those before we tend to strive on
with the bang of our gong and the rise of the sun
we fight for not only us, our peers
      our generation
but also for those before us
      who paved our way with words
      Kerouac, Rimbaud
      Selby Jr., Ginsberg
forefathers of american art
some of them are gone
yet their words still shine, always will
to the end of ours and your time
everyday someone new picks up a pen
and for that person a new world begins
a world of expression
      surrealism, and then
of mysticism, existentialism
      diarism, and then
a new face, fresh and forlorn to flow out their feelings
through ink from a pen
thinking of this i always choke
i'm no one, i know this but i'm no one who wrote
my words may be trivial
may rhyme or may not

perhaps i don't put a period or dot
for the rest of the days existence has left
my words will be carried along without jest
and if everything i've said or will say is gone
maybe one line will survive and live on
in the back of a matchbook,
        a mind or a throat

"i am no one, no one who wrote."

beat

finished reading Burroughs' <u>Junky</u>
something about 'h' attracts me
almost makes me wanna try and get a taste
form a habit
junkies can always tell the coolest stories
after they've came off a nod of course
they were always doing something
when not on a nod
        robbing, mugging
        lush working
        dropping bennies, drinking codeine
always passing the time
to me that sounds like fun
i should get hooked
become a junky
see if i can break my habit
then i can be like the greats
        Burroughs, Carroll, Nowell

or i could be myself

... and justice for all

we live in a place where we are raised
to think we are gods, invincible, indestructible
never caring about our past
never caring about our future
crime and poverty doesn't cross our minds
only money and possessions
in our country we think we rule the world
thinking all other countries worship us
sometimes we are proven wrong
we are wrong
we never acknowledge how important we are not
until we are knocked off our cloud by terrorists
wall street business is dead
consumerism is dead, for now
our city that never sleeps is unconscious
kings of business covered in dust
it is not deserved or condoned
but it is not that surprising
the world is not rational
the world is not civilized
it is irrational
    uncivilized
childhood is now over
        for thousands of kids today
they now see the true world
      a savage world
and we must pay for that
        with their innocence and our blood

[- written 9/11/2001 -]

just to piss off tripsy

it has been a long time
since i first looked in your eyes
    and saw the beauty
    and your love for me
feeling that hole in me
    filling with your heart
looking at you
    knowing it will be okay

it is amazing how
    i can still see and feel
    that after two years
still as strong
    or even stronger

i love you

[previously unreleased]

stayge evilootiun

i do not like these things i do
they hurt me more than help
sometimes i justify them based on stupidity
and allow it to continue
lying to myself
while killing myself with those lies
and all i ask is why?
you can't tell me it's just how i am
see i know that that is bullshit
to be honest i don't care anymore
usually i only feel bad because i know i'm supposed to
even when i'm glad i did what i did
seems to me that i am happy not being happy
doesn't matter anyway
all i do is talk about changes
yet i never do anything to change
and i piss and moan and bitch
thinking it will all be different someday
my day will come when i see the real darkness inside
yes, i will feel the true me
however dark it may seem now is only a preparation
one day it will overrun my body and mind and kill me
until then i will keep on this fucked-up track
shitting on myself and my history
enjoying every second

self-titled

i remember when i was young
before all of the backyards were fenced
and the neighbors took time to learn your name
running all day playing guns or tag
carrying a whiffle ball bat
       thinking i was Luke Skywalker
the days were so fresh
the air was so pure
like all of us young playing kids
when boys were boys
girls were girls
when color never mattered
watching 'Thundercats' or 'Voltron'
       'Transformers' and 'Heathcliff'
       'Jayce and the Wheeled Warriors'
       and 'M.A.S.K.'
never thinking about the passage of time
never thinking of what we will eventually lose
it was a time of joy and purity
       innocence and love
       being young and free
       awaiting it all
the calm before the storm
       playing, not knowing
       playing, yeah, playing
i was a child then ...

       ... 'til the streetlights came on

Series One _(1998 to 2006)_

'til the streetlights came on
understanding thursday
ars gratia artis
... for the minutes ...
in lucem proferre ...
... de nocte
x-rated
corruptio optimi pessima
reality vs. perception

Series Two _(2007)_

White Lies & the Confusion of Day Dreams
Black Truth & the Comprehension of Nightmares
Gray Days & the Possibility of Loveless Eyes
Golden Dust & the Resurgence of Youthful Trysts
Magenta Scars & the Delusions of Erudite Whores
Violet Dust & the Detriment of Broken Homes
Green Dreams & the Overflow of Orchidaceous Nights
Silver Rays & the Revolution of Dystopic Cliques
Cyan Lines & the Metamorphosis of Cyclical Tales

Series Three _(2008 to 2012)_

Junkyard Robot
In A World Of Reverse
A Treatise On Repose ...
See The Whole Board
Hums In Hollow Heads
270 Days Later
402 Roosevelt
24 Highway
10-14

Collections - Selected

iJihad
iKnew
iZobot
iFade

Collections - Complete

3,002 Days
Of An Example Made
Mind Shards
Fiber Scars

ISBN 979-8-89379-370-3